Today is a Rainy Day

by Martha E. H. Rustad

raintree 🍃

a Capstone company — publishers for children

Raintree is an imprint of Capstone Global Library Limited, a company incorporated in England and Wales having its registered office at 264 Banbury Road, Oxford, OX2 7DY – Registered company number: 6695582

www.raintree.co.uk
myorders@raintree.co.uk

Edited by Marissa Kirkman
Designed by Charmaine Whitman and Peggie Carley
Picture research by Tracey Engel
Production by Katy LaVigne
Originated by Capstone Global Library
Printed and bound in China.

ISBN 978 1 4747 3874 3
20 19 18 17 16
10 9 8 7 6 5 4 3 2 1

British Library Cataloguing in Publication Data
A full catalogue record for this book is available from the British Library.

Acknowledgements
We would like to thank the following for permission to reproduce photographs: iStockphoto: Chalabala, 10, emholk, 1, 16, Foxtrot101, 20, kozmoat98, 18 (top); Shutterstock: Arisa_J, 8, Dark Moon Pictures, 12, Dudarev Mikhail, 6, Kseniia Neverkovska, cover and interior design element, Michael C. Gray, cover, Tancha, cover and interior design element, TinnaPong, 4, VanderWolf Images, 14

Every effort has been made to contact copyright holders of material reproduced in this book. Any omissions will be rectified in subsequent printings if notice is given to the publisher.

All the internet addresses (URLs) given in this book were valid at the time of going to press. However, due to the dynamic nature of the internet, some addresses may have changed, or sites may have changed or ceased to exist since publication. While the author and publisher regret any inconvenience this may cause readers, no responsibility for any such changes can be accepted by either the author or the publisher.

Contents

What is the weather like?

Today is a rainy day.

Raindrops patter on the window.

Let's find out how much it will rain.

We check the forecast.

The sky is cloudy on a rainy day.

Dark clouds are full

of tiny drops of water.

When the water gets too heavy,

rain falls from the clouds.

The Water Cycle

condensation

precipitation

evaporation

ground water

Rain brings water to rivers, lakes and seas. Plants need water to grow. Their roots take in water from the ground. Animals need water, too. They drink water.

What do we see?

We see raindrops fall. We see water on the road. Puddles form on the pavement. Raindrops fall in lakes. We see tiny waves travel out from each drop.

We see lightning flash.

Then we hear thunder boom.

Thunderstorms have heavy rain,

lightning and thunder. Lightning

is electricity formed in clouds.

Too much rainfall can lead to a flood.

Lakes rise. Rivers overflow.

A flood forecast tells how much

the water will rise.

We stay away from flooded roads.

What do we do?

Let's splash in puddles!

We carry umbrellas. We wear raincoats and welly boots.

We go inside if we see lightning or hear thunder.

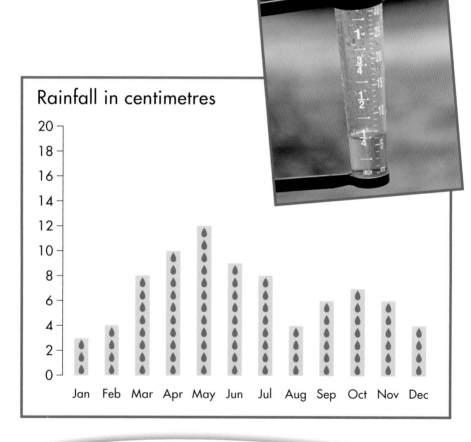

Rainfall in centimetres

We watch rain collect in the rain gauge. It tells us how much rain has fallen. We keep track on a chart. We see a pattern. Spring has many rainy days.

The rain stops.

The sun shines again.

We look for a rainbow.

Let's check tomorrow's forecast!

Glossary

flood   overflow of water from rivers and lakes

forecast   prediction of what the weather will be

lightning   electricity that forms in clouds

pattern   several things that are repeated in the same way each time

rain gauge   a narrow cup used to measure how much rain has fallen

Find out more

Books

Spring (Seasons), Stephanie Turnbull (Franklin Watts, 2015)

The Water Cycle (Fact Cat: Science), Izzi Howell (Wayland, 2016)

When Will It Rain?: Noticing Weather Patterns (Nature's Patterns), Martha E. H. Rustad (Millbrook Press, 2015)

Websites

www.bbc.co.uk/guides/z3wpp39
Learn about the water cycle.

climatekids.nasa.gov
Learn about the Earth's climate with games and videos.

www.weatherwizkids.com/weather-rain.htm
Learn all about rain and find directions to perform your own rain experiments.

Index

Note to parents and teachers

The What is the Weather Today? series supports National Curriculum requirements for science related to weather. This book describes and illustrates a rainy day. The images support early readers in understanding the text. The repetition of words and phrases helps early readers learn new words. This book also introduces early readers to subject-specific vocabulary words, which are defined in the Glossary section. Early readers may need assistance to read some words and to use the Contents, Glossary, Find out more and Index sections of the book.